# THE NEW IMPERIAL EDITION

# MEZZO-SOPRANO SONGS

*Compiled, Edited and Arranged by*
## SYDNEY NORTHCOTE

BOOSEY & HAWKES

AN IMAGEM COMPANY

DISTRIBUTED BY

HAL•LEONARD®
CORPORATION
7777 W. BLUEMOUND RD. P.O. BOX 13819 MILWAUKEE, WI 53213

# FOREWORD

THE NEW IMPERIAL EDITION OF SOLO SONGS has been designed as a chronological anthology of song from the Lutenists down to the present day. As other albums will be devoted exclusively to operatic and oratorio arias these are generally omitted from the present volumes.

Manifestly, the selection must be indicative rather than comprehensive or merely exclusive and is essentially practical, not personal. Each song is briefly annotated and, except where indicated, appears in the original key or is set for the voice with which it is normally associated.

Apart from obvious restrictions, the choice has been largely determined by certain positive needs. To provide the singing teacher and student alike with a working catalogue as a basis for more specialised research into the varied treasures of the literature of song ; to give to festival committees and examination bodies a ready way of governing without unduly restricting the dangerous freedom of own choice classes ; to present the would-be-accompanist with a convenient means of studying the many-sided aspects of his exacting technique ; and, lastly, to offer to all singers, whether amateur or professional, a practical and logical conspectus of the diversities of lyrical song over a period of some three hundred years. If, in addition, these books will do something to combat the present-day weakness for vocal exhibitionism or narrow eclecticism the labour of their preparation will be doubly justified.

*Croydon 1949*                                       SYDNEY NORTHCOTE

# INDEX

# ALPHABETICAL INDEX

# WHO EVER THINKS OR HOPES OF LOVE

Taken from Dowland's *First Booke of Songs or Ayres*
(1597) where it appears a tone higher. The poem is by Fulke
(Greville), Lord Brooke. For convenience sake, a purely arbi-
trary 2/2 time signature here replaces the irregular barring
of the original; but the singer must remember that the bar-lines
are meant for the eye and not the ear. All expression marks
are editorial suggestions.

JOHN DOWLAND
Original Lute accompaniment
adapted for piano by
SYDNEY NORTHCOTE

Who ever thinks or hopes of love for love,        Or who be-
Who thinks that sor - rows felt de-sires..... hid-den        Or hum-ble

- loved in Cu-pid's laws doth glo-ry        Who joys in vows,        or vows not to re-
faith in con-stant honour arm-éd        Can keep love from        the fruit that is for-

- move,        Who by........ this light god        hath not..... been made sor - ry,
- bid-den        Who thinks...that change is        by en - treat - y.... charm-éd,

Let him see        me        e - clips-éd from        my sun        With dark clouds of an
Look-ing on me        let        him know love's de - lights        Are trea-sures hid in

earth, with dark clouds of an earth quite o - ver - run.        run.
caves, are trea-sures hid in caves but kept .... by............ sprites.        sprites.

# LET ME LINGER NEAR THEE
## (Star Vicino)

Salvator Rosa (1615-1673), poet, painter and musician, wrote several solo songs with *basso continuo* accompaniment, many of which were published in the 'Gemme d'antichita.' The following, edited by Callcott, is a charming example of his suave melodiousness.

**English words by**
**MAY BYRON**

**Music by**
**SALVATOR ROSA**

Let me ling - er near thee for e - ver, In a vi - sion of
Star vi - ci - no al bel i - dol che s'a - ma, È il più va - go di -

rap - ture di - vine, Ah! what dark - - - - - -
- let - to... d'a - mor! È il più va - - - - -

- ness should se - ver My spi - rit from thine, should
- go di - let - to, di - let - to d'a - mor, Più
il_ più me - sto, più_

B. & H. **17130**

# NYMPHS AND SHEPHERDS

This delightful song— an excellent example of Purcell's pastoral music–comes from *The Libertine* (1692), where it appears a tone higher. It has earned an immortality which has been rightly denied to Shadwell's strange version of *Don Juan*.

Words by
**THOMAS SHADWELL**

Music by
**HENRY PURCELL**
Accompaniment by
**MYLES B. FOSTER**

grove, in this grove let's sport and play, let's sport and play, let's sport and play! For

this, this is Flo-ra's ho-ly day, this is Flo-ra's ho-ly day, this is

Flo-ra's ho-ly.... day!   Sa-cred to ease................................................................

...... and hap-py love,   To dancing, to mu - - sic, to

dan-cing,   to mu - - - - - - - - - sic and to po-et-ry.

Your flock may now, now, now, now, now, now, now, now, now, now se - cure - ly...

rove,......... Whilst you ex - press, whilst you ex - press.................

................your jol - li - ty!

Nymphs and shep - herds, come a - way, come a - way, Nymphs and shepherds,

come a - way, come a - way, come, come, come, come a - way!

# I ATTEMPT FROM LOVE'S SICKNESS TO FLY

This graceful *rondo* is one of Zempoalla's songs from *The Indian Queen* (1695), a play to which Dryden apparently contributed. A version was also printed in Orpheus Britannicus in the key of A but with two sharps only in the key signature.

Words by
Sir ROBERT HOWARD

Music by
HENRY PURCELL

I at-tempt from love's sick-ness to fly............ in... vain, Since I am my-self my own fe-ver, since I am my-self my own fe-ver, and pain. No more now, no more now fond... heart With pride no more

B. & H. 17180

swell, Thou canst not... raise for - ces, thou canst not raise for - ces e -

- nough to re - bel, I at - tempt from love's sick - ness to fly.....................

............. in .... vain, Since I am my - self my own fe - ver, since

I am my - self my own fe - ver and pain. For love has more power, and less

*This is given as D flat in Orpheus Britannicus

# ANGELS, EVER BRIGHT AND FAIR

This famous aria is taken from *Theodora* (1749) which was one of Handel's favourite oratorios.   Except for the firs. impassioned phrase, the recitative calls for a quiet declamation as a fitting prelude to the serene faith so beautifully expressed in the aria.

Dr CHARLES MORELL

Music by
G. F. HANDEL

# HERE AMID THE SHADY WOODS

*Alexander Balus* (1747) may not be among 'the perma-
nent successes of Handel's creations.' But it contains some
graceful and effective numbers of which this charming
pastoral is an exquisite example.

Dr CHARLES MORELL

Music by
G.F. HANDEL
Edited and arranged by
WALTER FORD and
RUPERT ERLEBACH

Here a - mid the sha - dy woods, Fra-grant flowers and crys - tal floods, Taste, my soul, this charming seat, Love and glo - ry's calm re-

B. & H. **17130**

- treat, ............ Taste, my soul, this charm - ing

seat, ....... Love and glo - ry's calm re - treat.

Here a - mid the sha - dy woods, ........

Taste, my soul, this charm - ing seat, Love and glo - ry's calm re -

- treat. ............ Here a - mid the sha - dy

# DRYADS, SYLVANS

## (from "Time and Truth")

*Time and Truth,* originally set by Handel to an Italian text in Rome (1708) was produced in London in 1737 and again, to an English version by Dr. Morell in 1757, when this song was among the many new additions. It is said to be the last work "on which Handel (in his blindness) was engaged."

Words by
D.ʳ MORELL

Music by
G.F. HANDEL
Edited and arranged by
WALTER FORD and
RUPERT ERLEBACH

Dry-ads, Syl-vans, with fair Flo-ra,

Dry-ads, Syl-vans, with fair

Flo-ra, Come, a-dorn this joy-ful place,

B.& H. 17130

...........come, a-dorn this joy-ful place! .......................

Dry-ads, Syl-vans, come, a - dorn, come, a-dorn..................this

joy - ful place! ...............................................

Dry-ads, Syl - - - - - vans,

Dry - ads, Syl-vans, with fair Flo - ra, come,................ a-dorn,...........

place,.................. this joy - ful place!

Come, fair I - ris, come,.... Au - ro - ra,

Come, fair I - ris, come,........ Au - ro - ra,

This our fes - ti - val.... to grace, this our fes - ti - val... to grace, ............ our fes - ti - val, ......... ...... come, fair I - ris, come, Au - ro - ra, come, Au - ro - - - - - - - - - - ra, this our

Adagio

a tempo

fes - ti - val.... to grace.

D. %

D. %

# WHEN DAISIES PIED

This was one of the delightful songs which Arne wrote for the revival of Shakespeare's *As you like it* in 1738. It has become almost inseparably associated with the verses.

Words by
WILLIAM SHAKESPEARE

Music by
THOMAS AUGUSTUS ARNE

Edited and arranged by
SYDNEY NORTHCOTE

When
When

dai - sies pied and vio - lets blue, And la - dy-smocks all sil - ver white, And
shep-herds pipe on oa - ten straws, And mer - ry larks are plough-men's clocks, And

cro - cus birds of yel - low hue, Do paint the mea - dows with de - light.
tur - tles tread, and rooks and daws, And mai - dens bleach their sum - mer frocks.

B. & H. 17130

# MY MOTHER BIDS ME BIND MY HAIR

This much-beloved song of Haydn is taken from his first set of Six Original Canzonettas written in England to English words and published by Corri, Dussek & Co in 1792-93. Mrs. Hunter was the wife of John Hunter, the famous surgeon and anatomist.

Words by
ANNE HUNTER

Music by
JOSEPH HAYDN

My mo - ther bids me bind my hair... With bands.... of.... ro - sy
'Tis sad..... to.... think the days are gone, When those..... we... love are

hue; Tie up........ my sleeves with ri - bands rare,.... And
near, I sit........ up - on this mos - sy stone,... And

lace my bo - dice blue,
sigh when none can hear,

Tie up....my sleeves with ri - bands
I sit... up - on this mos - sy

rare, And lace,.... and lace my.... bo - dice blue.
stone, And sigh,.... and sigh when none can hear.

"For why," she cries, "sit still and weep, While
And while I spin my flax - en thread, And

o - thers dance and play?"
sing my sim - ple lay,

A -
The

# NOW THE DANCING SUNBEAMS PLAY
## (The Mermaid's Song)

This is the second of Haydn's Six Original Canzonettas
written in England to English words and first published
in 1792-3. The accompaniment is more significant than
in his earlier German songs although he obviously thinks
orchestrally rather than in terms of the piano.

Music by
JOSEPH HAYDN

Now the........ danc - ing sun - beams play......
Come, be - hold what trea - sures lie ........

B. & H. 17130

# THE VIOLET
## (Das Veilchen)

JOH. WOLFGANG von GOETHE
English words by
SYDNEY NORTHCOTE

Although the writing of solo songs was never a matter of great importance with Mozart, there is no doubt that in this charming version of Goethe's poem can be seen the source of the modern Lied, and it remains as one of the earliest masterpieces in that form.

Music by
W. A. MOZART
Edited and arranged by
SYDNEY NORTHCOTE

B. & H. 17180

danced and sang so.... mer - ri - ly.
*-her, die Wie - se.... her und.... sang.*

"Ah" said the vio - let,.....
*"Ach" denkt das Veil - chen*

"were I.... now of all the flowers the one so fair that, she ......... might stoop to
*"wär' ich nur die schön-ste Blu - me der Na - tur ach! nur ......... ein klei - nes*

pluck me; Were I by her soft lips ca - ressed And to her bo - som
*Weil - chen, bis mich das Lieb - chen ab - gepflückt und an dem Bu - sen*

gent - ly pressed, 'Twould be for me a bliss - ful, heav'n - ly hour.
*matt ge - drückt, ach nur, ach nur ein Vier - tel - stünd - chen lang.*

Ah! but a - las! the mai-den gay Stepped all un-
*Ach, a - ber ach! das Mäd-chen kam und nicht in*

-heed-ing on her way, and crushed ......... the hap-less vio-let, It sank its
*Acht das Veil-chen nahm, er-trat ............ das ar-me Veil-chen. Es sank und*

head with gen-tle sigh: "If die I must, for her I die, for
*starb und freut' sich noch: und sterb' ich den, so sterb' ich doch durch*

her, for her, ............. as at her feet I ..... lie"
*sie, durch sie, ............. zu ih-ren Fü - - ssen doch"*

Poor fa-ded vio-let! It was the sweet-est vio-let!
*Das ar - me Veil-chen! es war ein her-zig's Veil-chen!*

# KNOW'ST THOU THE LAND

## (Kennst du das Land)

JOH. WOLFGANG von GOETHE
English words by
JOHN OXENFORD

This beautiful poem stands at the head of the third book of *Wilhelm Meister* and has inspired several masterly settings although the strange spirit of *Mignon* is not easy to capture. Beethoven wrote this in 1810, the year of *Egmont*.

Music by
L. van BEETHOVEN

# DEEP IN MY HEART

Sir Henry Rowley Bishop (1786-1855) was the first
musician to be knighted by Queen Victoria. At its
best, his vocal music has a certain haunting quality
as this expressive song reveals.

Music by
HENRY ROWLEY BISHOP
Arranged and Edited by
ALEC ROWLEY

B. & H. 17130

mine, 'Till thou say'st "I love thee", thou say'st I.... love thee; 'Till thou say'st "I love thee

tru - ly, tru - ly, tru - ly," Will I....give my...heart to thee.

Deep in.... my.... heart.....thou art........ my trea-sure

rare,........ Thou hast my........ love,..... None ............with thee can com -

# THE WILD ROSE

## (Heiden Röslein)

JOH. WOLFGANG von GOETHE
English words by
M. X. HAYES

Written in 1815, this beautifully articulated melody is so natural that it might have been born with the verses which Goethe wrote in 1771. It is here transposed a minor third lower.

Music by
FRANZ SCHUBERT

Thought-less-ly he pulled the rose, In the hedge-row grow-ing;
*Und der wil-de Kna-be... brach's, Rös-lein auf der Hei-den;*

*p*

But her thorns their spears op-pose, Vain-ly he la-ments his woes, With
*Rös-lein wehr-te sich... und stach, half ihr doch kein Weh und Ach,*

*rit.*

pain his... hand is.... glow-ing. Lit-tle wild rose, wild rose red,
*musst' es.... e-ben lei-den. Rös-lein, Rös-lein, Rös-lein roth,*

*cresc.* *pp* *rit.*

*a tempo*

In the hedge-row grow-ing.
*Rös-lein auf der Hei-den.*

*a tempo*

# CRADLE SONG

### (Wiegenlied)

MATTHAIS CLAUDIUS
English words by
M.X.HAYES

Written in 1816, this charming lullaby has been aptly
described by Capell as "the very paragon of cradle songs."
Richard Strauss quotes the melody in his opera *Ariadne
auf Naxos*.

Music by
FRANZ SCHUBERT

Slum - ber, slum - ber, dear-est, sweet-est trea-sure, Rocked so gent - ly
*Schla - fe, schla - fe, hol - der, süss - er Kna - be, lei - se wiegt dich*

by thy mo-ther's hand; Soft re - pose and tran-quil plea-sure Soothe thee with... the
*dei - ner Mut - ter Hand; sanf - te Ru - he, mil - de La - be bringt dir schwe-bend*

lull-ing cra-dle band. Slum-ber, slum-ber,
*dies - es Wie-gen-band. Schla - fe, schla - fe*

in sweet dreams re - pos - ing, While pro - tects...thee thy fond mo-ther's arm,
*in dem süss - en....Gra - be, noch be - schützt dich dei - ner Mut - ter Arm;*

B. & H. 17180

All her rich-es, here... en-clos-ing, Hold she in..... her clasp so true and warm.
*al - le Wün-sche, al - le Ha-be fasst sie lie-bend, al-le lie-be-warm.*

Slum - ber, slum - ber
*Schla - fe, schla - fe*

*pp*

on thy down-y.... pil - low, Love's hymn round thee mu-sic sweet shall make;
*in der Flau-men Schoos-se, noch um - tönt....dich lauter Lie-bes - ton,*

And a li - ly and...... a rose-bud Shall re - ward..... thee
*ei - ne Li - lie, ei - ne Ro - se, nach dem Schla - fe*

when thou dost a - wake.
*werd' sie dir... zum Lohn.*

# PEACE

### (Du bist die Ruh')

FRIEDRICH RÜCKERT
English words by
M.X. HAYES

In all, Schubert set five poems by Rückert (1788-1866) and this one, written in 1823 is a challenge to artistic integrity as well as vocal skill. It wants a perfect *mezza voce*; and the long phrases are in themselves a delicate technical problem.

Music by
FRANZ SCHUBERT

PIANO
*pp*

Thou art sweet Peace and tran-quil rest, I long for thee to
*Du bist die Ruh', der Frie-de mild, die Sehn-sucht du, und*

*pp*

soothe my breast; I de-di-cate,........ 'mid joys and...sighs,
*was sie stillt; ich wei-he dir............ voll Lust und Schmerz,*

Thy dwell-ing in............ my heart and eyes,........ my heart and eyes,........
*zur Woh-nung hier............ mein Aug' und Herz,........ mein Aug' und Herz.........*

* Friedländer gives both these notes as D flat. *The Editor*

# THE BRIDE'S SONG
## (Lied der Braut)

FRIEDRICH RÜCKERT
English words by
M.X. HAYES

One of the *Myrthenlieder* which Schumann wrote as a bridal gift for Clara in 1840, this song has a quiet intensity which must never be allowed to become sentimental.

Music by
ROBERT SCHUMANN

thee............ I owe, Life to me thou didst im-part, That I love's
*erst ............ dich sehr, dass du mir das Seyn ver-lich'n, das mir*

bliss on earth should know, That I love's bliss.......... on earth should
*ward zu sol-chem Glanz, das..... mir ward zu sol-chem, sol-chem*

know.
*Glanz.*

Adagio

# SOMEBODY
## (Jemand)

W. GERHARD
English words by
ROBERT BURNS

Another of the *Myrthenlieder* to which the original poem by Burns is easily adapted. Passionate, almost wilful, there is a graphic intensity in Schumann's declamation which calls for a studied judgement in the changes of tempo.

Music by
ROBERT SCHUMANN
Edited and arranged by
SYDNEY NORTHCOTE

B. & H. 17130

# IN A STRANGE LAND

(In der Fremde)

H. von FALLERSLEBEN
English words by
CONSTANCE BACHE

Wilhelm Taubert (1811-1891) was much praised by
Mendelssohn but only a few graceful songs are now remembered of his large catalogue of compositions.

Music by
WILHELM TAUBERT

old, But I....shall ne - ver - more be-hold Their sweet - ness past com
*-her, ich a - ber se - he sie nicht mehr, und fra - ge sie auch*

- pare; "O flowers, how sweet so - e'er ye be, Your
*nie. Was seht ihr an mein Schät - ze - lein? Von*

beau - ty is but pale to me Be - side my love so fair:" For
*Euch kann kei - nes schö - ner sein, keins schö - ner sein als sie: Mein*

fair........................ as day was she, For
*hol - - - - - - - des Schät - ze - lein, mein*

fair as day was she! For fair........
*sü - sses Schät - ze - lein! Mein hol - - - - -*

*dolce sotto voce*

as day... was she, For fair as day was she!
*- - des Schät - ze - lein, mein sü - sses Schät - ze - lein!*

dolce sotto votto

And still the trees their sha - dows spread, But I... to dis - tant
*Noch steht der Baum im Tha - le dort, ich a - ber zog zur*

lands have fled, For one dear place is bare; A stran-ger on an a - lien
*Frem - de fort; und leer ist je - ner Platz. Ich sitz' auf ö - dem, kal - tem*

shore, That loved spot I shall see no more, For she no more is
*Stein, Ich sitz' hier in der Fremd' al - lein, und denk' an mei - nen*

# SPRING'S SECRET

## (Der Frühling)

J.B. ROUSSEAU
English words by
PAUL ENGLAND

Written in April 1852, this is a typical Brahms-Hungarian song. The poet— in his youth an associate of Heine—was proud enough to acknowledge, in the 1866 edition of his poetry, settings by Reissiger and Weiss; apparently he did not know of this far greater setting by Brahms!

Music by
JOHANNES BRAHMS

B. & H. 17130

clouds a - part, And per - fume all the for - est's
*sanft und lau, Ge - schau - kelt in dem Wol - ken -*

heart, Like heaven - ly cen - sers swing - ing,
*- bau, Wie Him - mels - duft......... her - nie - der,*

Like heaven - ly cen - sers swing - ing. From
*Wie Him - mels - duft......... her - nie - der. Da*

fold - ed sheath the flowers a - wake, While am-'rous birds in bush and brake.......................
*wer - den al - le Blu - men wach, Da tönt der Vö - gel schmel-zend Ach!...........................*

...... Of...... Spring's re - turn are sing - ing, Of........
*...... Da...... kehrt der Früh - ling wie - der, Da........*

Spring's re - turn are sing - - ing.
*kehrt der Früh-ling wie - - der.*

*mf con espressione*

*dim. sost.*

*p dolce ed espressivo*

From cup to cup, from spray to spray, The
*Es weht der Wind den Blü-then-staub Von*

*p*

*p dolce*

blos - som dust by night and day Is
*Kelch zu Kelch, von Laub zu Laub, Durch*

*p*

waft - ed, white..... and yel - low, Is waft - ed,
*Ta - ge und........ durch Näch - te, Durch Ta - ge*

*p*

*f*

*p*

white........ and yel - low.
und ........... durch Näch - te.

Thou too, my heart, be-
Flieg' auch, mein Herz, und

- gin thy quest! Seek here and there, till in some breast .............................. Thou
flat - tere fort, Such' hier ein Herz und such' es dort, ............................... Du.....

find, per-chance,thy fel - low,
triffst viel-leicht das Rech - te,

Thou find, per-chance, thy
Du triffst viel - leicht das

fel - - low!
Rech - - te.

# THE BLACKSMITH
## (Der Schmied)

LUDWIG UHLAND
English words by
PAUL ENGLAND

There are innumerable settings of this poem all of
which have been utterly supplanted by this most popular
of all Brahms' songs. It should be remembered that
Allegro means lively rather than fast.

Music by
JOHANNES BRAHMS

My true love is there! His ham - mer's a -
*Ich hör' mei - nen Schatz, Den Ham - mer er*

- swing - ing, His an - vil is ring - ing With strokes thick - ly
*schwin - get, Das rau - schet, das klin - get, Das dringt in die*

fall - ing, Like bells clear - ly call - ing Through al - - -
*Wei - te Wie Glo - cken - ge - läu - te, Durch Gas - - -*

- ley and square.
*- sen und Platz.*

B. & H. 17130

I pass by the place, And then, as he sees me, My
*Am schwar-zen Ka - min,* *Da sit - zet mein Lie - ber, Doch,*

dar - ling, to please me, Sets bel - lows a - roar - ing, And flames, up - ward
*geh' ich vor - ü - ber, Die Bäl - ge dann sau - sen Die Flam - men auf-*

*cresc.*

soar - ing, Light up............................................ his dear face!
*- brau - sen, Und lo - - - dern um ihn.*

# PARTING

## (Muss es eine Trennung)

LUDWIG TIECK
English words by
PAUL ENGLAND

This is № 12 of the *Magelone* song cycle which
Brahms published in two parts; Nos.1-6 in 1862 and
the remainder in 1869. Variants in the German text
are shewn in brackets.

Music by
JOHANNES BRAHMS

B. & H. 17130

pain.
*nicht.*

Shep - - herd's pi - ping, soft... and ten - der,
*Hör'............ ich ei - nes Schä - fers Flö - te,*

Speaks ............ of grief and loss..... to me;
*här - - me ich.... mich in - nig - lich,*

Skies ............ a - glow... with sun - set splen - dour
*seh'............ ich in........ die A - bend - rö - - the,*

Wring ............ my heart with thoughts of thee.
*denk'............ ich brün - stig - lich..... an dich.*

# ORPHEUS WITH HIS LUTE

Words by
**WILLIAM SHAKESPEARE**

There is a characteristic freshness in this, one of the most popular of Sullivan's Shakespearean songs. Some literary scholars consider the poem to be the work of John Fletcher.

Music by
**ARTHUR SULLIVAN**

Or - pheus with his lute, with his lute made trees And the

moun - tain tops that freeze Bow.......... themselves when he ............ did

sing: Or - - - - - - pheus with his

*a tempo*  *cresc.*

heart,............... In sweet mu - - sic

is ......... such art, .................... Kill - ing care ......... and...

*un poco più lento*

grief of heart Fall..... a - sleep, or hear - ing,

die, Fall a - sleep, or hear - - - - ing, or

*lunga pausa*

hear - ing, die.

# THE UNDISCOVERED COUNTRY
## (L'île inconnue)

THÉOPHILE GAUTIER
English words by
PAUL ENGLAND

There is nothing of the Berlioz eccentricities in his songs; but something of his influence on the subsequent development of French song will be discovered in this effective setting of Gautier's well-known poem.

Music by
HECTOR BERLIOZ

Allegro spiritoso

PIANO

Tell me fair mai - den whi-ther a - way shall we go? Our
Di - tes, la jeu - ne belle, Où vou - lez vous al - ler? La

boat swelleth her sail ............. as the breeze be - gins to blow. Our
voi - le en-fle son ai - le, La bri - se va souf-fler, La

boat doth swell her sail ............ as the breeze be - gins ...............
voi - le en-fle son ai - le, La bri - se va ...............

rit.

tell me, whi - - ther, whither shall we go? "Let us
*bel - le, di - - tes, Où vou - lez vous al - ler?* "Me - nez

seek........ o'er the o - cean Some fair isle of de - vo - tion Where
*moi,"........ dit la bel - le "A la ri - ve fi - dè - le.... Où lo'n*

true love ............................. will last.... for aye!"
*ai - - - - - - - - me ..... tou - jours."*

"Such a land" said the lo - ver.... We shall ne - ver dis - co - ver,
*Cet - te ri - ve, ma chè - re,.... on ne la con - nait guè - re,*

Such a land said the lov - er, We shall
*Cet - te ri - ve, ma chè - re, on ne*

# SLUMBER SONG

## (Dors, mon enfant)

Anonymous
English words by
R. H. ELKIN

This was the first of the *Trois Mélodies* which
Wagner published in Paris in 1840. Blom has said that
"the music has a captivating charm mixed with a
certain monotony" while Minna Wagner thought it
"a lovely thing to send one to sleep."

Music by
RICHARD WAGNER

# TO THE CHILDREN
## (Aux enfants)

This is one of the most beautiful of Rachmaninoff's songs. It wants a smooth, fluent declamation and a restrained intensity in expression. The accompaniment, too, must have a perfect sostenuto and imaginative tone control.

M.D.CALVOCORESSI
English words by
ROSA NEWMARCH

Music by
SERGEI RACHMANINOFF

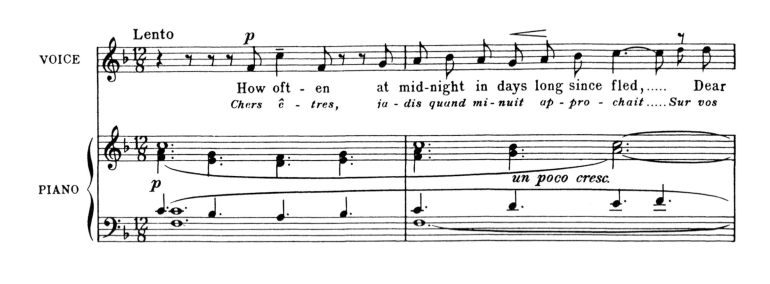

B. & H. 17130

*Dedicated to my wife*

# ALONE IN THE FOREST
## (Waldseligkeit)

RICHARD DEHMEL
English words by
PAUL ENGLAND

The intense quiet of this song, written in 1901, is
not easy to control, and if the molto lento of the con-
cluding phrase is to have its due effect, the rest of the
song must move easily and not too slowly.

Music by
RICHARD STRAUSS

B. & H. **17130**

# MELMILLO

Words by
**WALTER de la MARE**

All the songs of Clive Carey (b. 1883) show the
insight of a fine singer as well as a real musicianship,
as this, perhaps his finest song, so eloquently reveals.

Music by
**CLIVE CAREY**

B. & H. 17180

# DREAM VALLEY

Among the many charming songs which Roger Quilter (b. 1877) has contributed to the literature of English song there will always be a special place for the delicate serenity of this little masterpiece, which wants a sensitive understanding between singer and accompanist.

**Words by**
**WILLIAM BLAKE**

**Music by**
**ROGER QUILTER**

Me-mo-ry, hi-ther come, And tune your mer-ry notes; And, while up-on the wind Your

mu-sic floats, I'll pore up-on the stream Where sighing lov-ers dream, And

fish....for fancies as they pass With - in the wa-t'ry glass. I'll

B. & H. 17130

drink of... the clear stream, And hear the lin-net's song, And there I'll lie and dream The

day a-long; And, when night comes, I'll go To pla-ces fit for woe,.....

Walk-ing a-long the darkened val-ley With si-lent Me - lan - cho - ly.

# GIRLS' SONG

There is always a rare distinction in all that Dr. Herbert Howells (b. 1892) writes and the gracious buoyancy of this song is achieved by a perfectly natural vocal declamation set above a scintillating and sensitive pianoforte accompaniment.

Words by
**WILFRED WILSON GIBSON**

Music by
**HERBERT HOWELLS**

B. & H. **17130**

-turn-ing emp-ty from the fair Be-hind the old jog - trot-ting mare........

........ But it was-n't the re - turn-ing of a clat-t'ring, emp-ty cart, That

sent the hot blood burn - ing And throb-bing, throb-bing, throb-bing through my

heart.........................

# SOMEONE TO WATCH OVER ME

## "Oh, Kay!"

Music and Lyrics by
GEORGE GERSHWIN and IRA GERSHWIN